THE
TOTALLY
CORN
COOKBOOK

Printed in Singapore

The Totally Corn Cookbook is produced by becker&mayer!, Ltd.

Cover illustration and design: Dick Witt

Interior design and typesetting: Dona McAdam, Mac on the Hill

Library of Congress Cataloging-in-Publication Data:
Siegel, Helene.
          The totally corn cookbook / by Helene Siegel & Karen
Gillingham.
              p.   cm.
          ISBN 0-89087-726-2 ; $4.95
          1. Cookery (corn)   I. Gillingham, Karen. II. Title
TX809.M2554   1994   94-2127
641.6'567—dc20   CIP

Celestial Arts
PO Box 7123
Berkeley, CA 94707

Other cookbooks in this series:
The Totally Garlic Cookbook
The Totally Chile Pepper Cookbook
The Totally Mushroom Cookbook

THE TOTALLY CORN COOKBOOK

by Helene Siegel and Karen Gillingham
Illustrations by Ani Rucki

CELESTIAL ARTS
BERKELEY, CA

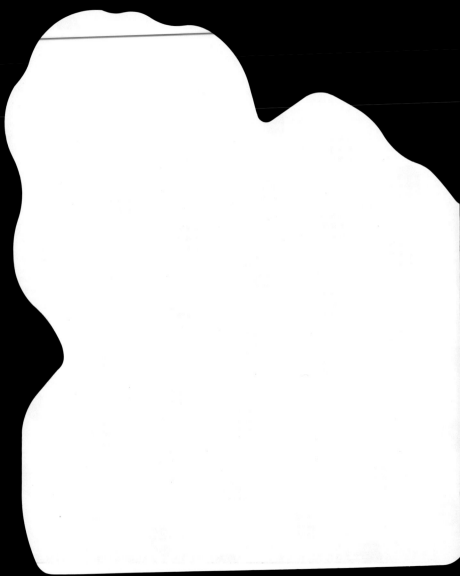

CONTENTS

"Corn has a pleasant flavor and all of the people of this country live on it."
                                              —Christopher Columbus

Of all the new foodstuffs Columbus discovered when he found the New World, none has had the impact of corn. Just try to imagine a world of wheat chips, popped wheat, and wheat whiskey and you will see what we mean.

In addition to the five hundred industrial uses that corn now has, it relentlessly feeds America and the world in the form of corn flakes and grits, breads, muffins, puddings, pancakes, tortillas, chips, tamales, polenta, hominy for stewing, starch for coating and thickening, oil for cooking, syrup for sweetening, and whiskey for sipping.

But most important—especially if you have children to feed—corn is the most accessible of vegetables. Who can resist it? The mere thought of corn makes grumps smile, think of sunnier days, and take out the butter.

Following, then, are some ideas for cooking with America's sweetheart. Here is a light, sweet soup of summer corn, one with an Asian dash of sesame, and a fabulous Mexican fish chowder. Here is spicy popcorn to knock your socks off, warm polenta, grits, and creamed corn to offer solace when oatmeal just won't do, sturdy golden breads sprinkled with fresh herbs or enriched with buttermilk for brightening the breakfast table, and a few elegant salads (with ingredients such as smoked turkey and lobster) for those who must maintain their slender figures while they eat their corn too.

Of course there are a few sweets for the truly corn obsessed. In addition to the best corncakes and waffles ever to meet a bottle of maple syrup, candied corn reaches new heights in crêpes, and in crème brûlée dotted with caramelized kernels of young, sweet corn. Bright orange Halloween corn will never taste the same! Best wishes for a happy corn season!

CONTENTS

SOOTHING SOUPS,
SOUPS,
BRIGHT SALADS
& PARTY FOODS

SWEET SUMMER CORN SOUP

4 tablespoons butter
1 onion, chopped
1 garlic clove, chopped
4 cups fresh corn kernels
2 cups chicken stock
2 cups half and half or milk
   Salt and freshly ground pepper
   Chopped fresh herbs such as
   tarragon, chives, parsley

Melt butter in medium pot over medium heat. Cook onions and garlic until soft, 5 minutes. Add corn and cook, stirring frequently, 8 minutes.

Transfer to food processor along with 1 cup of chicken stock. Purée until smooth and pour back into soup pot.

Pour in remaining chicken stock, half and half or milk, and salt and pepper. Cook over medium-low heat until nearly boiling, 15 minutes. Adjust seasonings and garnish with fresh herbs. Serve hot.

Serves 4 .

CORN IN AMERICAN INDIAN CULTURE

Corn was the primary food of all Indian people, except the nomadic tribes, who ate buffalo meat. Most Indians did not raise cattle or drink milk and were horrified when Europeans brought over their cows and let them graze on maize. To the Indians, corn was food fit for gods and man.

SHRIMP & CORN SOUP

1 pound medium shrimp
2 tablespoons butter
1/2 small onion, diced
1 celery rib, diced
2 jalapeños, stemmed, seeded, and diced
2 cups corn kernels
1 (14 1/2-ounce) can chicken broth
1 cup half and half
   Coarse salt
   Cilantro sprigs

Leaving tails intact on 4 to 6 shrimp, peel and devein remaining shrimp. Butterfly tail-on shrimp and chop remaining.

In large saucepan, melt butter. Add butterflied shrimp and sauté just until bright pink and cooked through. Set aside. Add onion, celery, and jalapeños to pan. Sauté until onion is tender. Stir in chopped shrimp and sauté just until bright pink. Add all but 1/4 cup corn and sauté 30 seconds longer. Add broth and half and half. Cook, stirring constantly, until smooth and heated through.

Serve in bowls, garnished with remaining corn kernels, butterflied shrimp, and cilantro sprigs.

Serves 4 to 6.

FRESH CORN SESAME SOUP

2 tablespoons butter
4 cups corn kernels
2 cups half and half
1 (14½-ounce) can chicken broth
¼ cup dry sherry
1 teaspoon sesame oil
   Coarse salt and freshly ground pepper
   Black sesame seeds (optional)
4 sprigs cilantro

In large saucepan, melt butter over medium heat.
Add corn and cook, stirring until evenly coated.
Stir in half and half and chicken broth and bring to
boil. Reduce heat and simmer 5 minutes. Transfer
mixture to blender in two batches and blend until
puréed. Return to pan and stir in sherry and
sesame oil. Season to taste with salt and pepper.
Serve in bowls garnished with black sesame
seeds, if desired, and cilantro.

Serves 4 to 6.

CORN & ZUCCHINI SOUP

Corn and squash were natural companions in the Indian garden.

2 tablespoons butter
1 onion, diced
2 garlic cloves, minced
4 small zucchinis, grated
2 cups corn kernels
2 medium tomatoes, seeded and diced
2 tablespoons shredded fresh basil
2 (10¾-ounce) cans condensed chicken broth
1 cup half and half
Dried red pepper flakes (optional)
Coarse salt and freshly ground pepper

In large saucepan, melt butter. Add onion and garlic and sauté over medium-high heat until soft. Add zucchini and cook, stirring frequently, about 2 minutes, until zucchini is barely tender. Stir in corn, tomatoes, basil, and chicken broth. Bring to boil. Reduce heat and simmer 5 minutes. Stir in half and half and simmer just until heated through. Season to taste with pepper flakes, if desired, and salt and pepper.

Serves 6.

HOMINY SALAD

1 (15-ounce) can white or golden hominy, rinsed
   and drained
2 medium tomatoes, chopped
1/2 red onion, minced
2 jalapeños, stemmed, seeded, and minced
1/2 cup chopped cilantro
1/4 cup sliced black olives
   Juice of 1 lime
   Coarse salt and freshly ground pepper
   Green leaf lettuce leaves
   Lime wedges

In bowl combine hominy, tomatoes, onion, jalapeños,
cilantro, and olives. Add lime juice and season to taste
with salt and pepper. Toss until well mixed. Serve on
individual salad plates lined with lettuce leaves and
garnished with lime wedges.

Serves 4.

THAI CORN BLACK BEAN SALAD

2 cups cooked corn kernels
1 (16-ounce) can black beans, rinsed and drained
1/2 cup diced celery
1/2 cup diced onion
1/2 cup diced red bell pepper
1/4 cup chopped fresh cilantro
1 to 2 jalapeños, stemmed, seeded, and minced
2 garlic cloves, minced
1 teaspoon minced fresh ginger
3 tablespoons sesame oil
2 tablespoons rice vinegar
1 tablespoon fresh lime juice
Coarse salt

In large bowl, combine corn, black beans, celery, onion, red bell, cilantro, jalapeño, garlic, and ginger.

In small bowl, whisk oil with vinegar and lime juice. Pour dressing over bean mixture and toss to combine. Season to taste with salt. Chill until serving time.

Serves 4.

CORN & JICAMA SALAD

  2 cups cooked corn kernels (preferably grilled)
  1 cup diced jicama
¼ cup sliced green onion
  1 avocado, peeled and cut in chunks
  1 red bell pepper, stemmed, seeded, and diced
  1 jalapeño, stemmed, seeded, and minced
    Juice of 1 lime
  1 tablespoon corn oil
    Coarse salt and freshly ground pepper
    Butter lettuce

In large bowl, combine corn, jicama, green onion,
avocado, red bell, jalapeño, lime juice, and oil.
Season to taste with salt and pepper. Toss thoroughly.
Serve on individual lettuce-lined plates.

Serves 4 to 6.

CORNCAKES WITH SMOKED SALMON

These little pancakes are stiff enough to be eaten out of hand with cocktails. If you prefer your cornmeal on the sweet side, try sprinkling each silver-dollar pancake with powdered sugar and topping with a dollop of your favorite jam.

1/2 cup yellow cornmeal
1/4 teaspoon salt
1/2 cup boiling water
 1 egg
1/4 cup milk
 4 tablespoons butter, melted
1/2 cup flour
 1 tablespoon baking powder
   Butter for coating
1/2 cup whipped cream cheese
 2 ounces thinly sliced smoked salmon
   Fresh dill sprigs or chives, sliced

Combine cornmeal and salt in large bowl. Pour in boiling water and stir well to evenly moisten.

In another bowl, whisk together egg, milk, and butter until well blended. Stir into cornmeal mixture.

In small bowl, stir flour and baking powder together with fork. Stir into cornmeal mixture until well blended.

Heat cast-iron skillet or griddle over medium-low heat. Lightly coat with butter. Drop batter by tablespoonfuls into pan and cook about 2 minutes per side, until golden all over. On second side, press with spatula to flatten slightly and adjust heat down if browning too quickly. Transfer to platter to cool in single layer.

Spread each with about 1 teaspoon whipped cream cheese. Cut salmon into 18 strips and place over cream cheese. Sprinkle with chives or dill and serve.

Makes 18.

SMOKED TURKEY ON CORN MINI-MUFFINS

Buttermilk Corn Muffins batter (see p.72)
3⁄4 teaspoon poultry seasoning
Smoked turkey slices
Coarse salt and freshly ground pepper
1⁄2 cup cranberry sauce

Preheat oven to 375 degrees F.

Prepare batter, adding poultry seasoning to dry ingredients. Spoon batter into 2 greased mini-muffin pans and bake 15 minutes. Turn out on rack to cool.

To assemble, cut muffins in half crosswise. Place a few slices turkey and 1 teaspoon cranberry sauce on each bottom. Enclose with top half and serve.

Makes 24.

SPICY POPCORN

This is an adaptation of chefs Mary Sue Milliken's and Susan Feniger's hot and spicy popcorn from City Restaurant in Los Angeles.

1/2 teaspoon paprika
1/2 teaspoon cayenne
1/2 teaspoon ground cumin
1 teaspoon salt
1/4 teaspoon black pepper
1/4 cup vegetable oil
1/2 cup unpopped corn

Measure out spices and keep nearby.

Place oil and one kernel popcorn in pot over high heat. Cover and wait for corn to pop. Then add popcorn and cover again. When corn starts popping, quickly add spices. Cover and cook, shaking constantly, until popping stops.

CONTENTS

CORN SALSAS,
RELISHES
& SIDES

COOL CORN SALSA

This refreshing summertime salsa is delicious alongside grilled flank steak, fish, or poultry. And for those who can never have too much of a good thing, it makes an excellent dip with fresh-fried corn chips.

3 cups corn kernels
2 Anaheims, roasted, peeled, seeded, and diced
1 red bell pepper, seeded and diced
3 tablespoons diced red onion
1 bunch fresh chives, sliced
1/4 cup red wine vinegar
1/2 cup olive oil
Salt, freshly ground pepper, and Tabasco to taste

Blanch corn kernels in boiling salted water until water returns to boil. Drain and rinse with cold water. Transfer to mixing bowl. Add Anaheim and red bell peppers, onion, and chives and mix.

In small bowl whisk together red wine vinegar, oil, salt, pepper, and 2 or 3 dashes Tabasco. Pour over corn mixture, toss well and serve room temperature or chill.

Makes 3 1/2 cups.

CORN & TOMATILLO RELISH

2 tablespoons oil
1 red bell pepper, stemmed, seeded, and minced
1/2 onion, minced
1 jalapeño, stemmed, seeded, and minced
2 cups corn kernels
1 (18-ounce) can tomatillos, drained and chopped
1/2 teaspoon ground coriander
1/2 teaspoon ground cumin
Coarse salt and freshly ground pepper

Heat oil in large skillet. Add red bell, onion, and jalapeño and sauté, stirring occasionally, until vegetables are soft. Stir in corn, tomatillos, coriander, and cumin and bring to boil. Reduce heat and simmer 5 minutes. Season to taste with salt and pepper. Serve warm or cold as side dish with grilled or roasted meats.

Makes about 3 1/2 cups.

GRILLED CORN SALSA

2 ears corn, husked
1 red onion, sliced ½-inch thick
4 Italian plum tomatoes
2 jalapeños, stemmed, seeded, and minced
½ cup chopped cilantro
Coarse salt and freshly ground pepper

Over medium-hot coals, grill corn, onion, and tomatoes until they begin to brown. Cut kernels from corn and chop onion slices and tomatoes. Combine corn, onion, tomatoes, jalapeños, and cilantro in bowl. Season to taste with salt and pepper. Serve room temperature or chilled with grilled chicken, fish, or meats or as topping for quesadillas, tacos, or tostadas.

Makes about 3 cups.

SAUTÉED CORN & PEPPERS

1 tablespoon olive oil
1 tablespoon butter
½ onion, chopped
  Salt and freshly ground pepper
½ teaspoon ground cumin
2 cups corn kernels
1 small poblano pepper, roasted, seeded, and peeled
1 red bell pepper, roasted, seeded, and peeled
1 tomato, seeded and chopped
  Juice of 1 lime

Heat oil and butter in large skillet over medium-high heat. Sauté onion with salt, pepper, and cumin until soft and golden, 5 minutes. Add corn and sauté 2 minutes longer.

Meanwhile finely chop poblano and roughly chop bell pepper. Add to corn mixture and cook another 3 minutes. Reduce heat, stir in tomatoes and lime juice. Adjust with salt and pepper and serve hot.

Serves 4.

HOMEMADE CREAMED CORN

2 tablespoons butter
3 cups fresh corn kernels
   Coarse salt and freshly ground pepper
¼ cup milk
¼ cup plus 2 tablespoons heavy cream
2 teaspoons each chopped fresh thyme and tarragon

Melt butter in medium skillet over medium heat. Sauté corn with salt and pepper 3 minutes. Pour in milk and ¼ cup cream, turn up heat, and boil until thick, about 5 minutes.

Transfer half to food processor or blender and pulse until chunky purée is formed. Pour back into the pan. Over low heat, stir in herbs and remaining cream. Season to taste with salt and pepper. Serve hot.

Serves 4.

MARTHA'S GRITS

This rich dish of grits, butter, and cheese, from a genuine
Southerner, is as versatile and delicious as any polenta.
Stir in diced ham, crumbled bacon, or even chopped
sun-dried tomatoes and forget about the calories.

4 cups cooked quick grits, hot
6 tablespoons butter, softened and cut into 6 pats
2 teaspoons salt
   Freshly ground black pepper
3 eggs, beaten
2 cups cheddar, Gruyère, or Parmesan or mixture

Preheat oven to 400 degrees F. Butter 9 by 13-inch
casserole.

   While grits are hot, stir in butter 1 tablespoon at a
time until melted. Add salt and pepper. Let cool slightly.
Slowly stir in beaten eggs. Mix in cheeses and spoon
into buttered pan. Bake 20 minutes, until slightly
golden and puffy. Serve hot.

Serves 6 to 8.

POLENTA WEDGES WITH PARMESAN & BASIL

1 cup dry polenta
1 cup milk
1 (14½-ounce) can chicken broth
3 tablespoons butter
1 cup corn kernels
½ cup grated Parmesan
2 tablespoons chopped fresh basil
  Coarse salt and freshly ground pepper
  Tomato sauce or salsa

In small bowl, blend polenta and milk. Set aside.

In heavy medium saucepan, bring chicken broth and butter to boil. Add polenta mixture all at once and return to boil, stirring constantly. Reduce heat, add corn, and simmer until very thick, stirring often, about 15 minutes. Stir in Parmesan, basil, and salt and pepper to taste.

Spoon hot mixture into 9-inch round cake pan and smooth top. Let cool, then refrigerate.

To serve, cut polenta into wedges and broil or grill until browned and heated through. Top with tomato sauce or salsa and serve with grilled chicken, sausages, or other meats.

Serves 6.

POLENTA WITH MASCARPONE & PORCINI

1 ounce dried porcini
1 cup warm water
2 tablespoons butter
1 small onion, minced
1 garlic clove, minced
Coarse salt and freshly ground pepper
1/2 (13-ounce) package instant polenta
4 ounces mascarpone cheese, room temperature
Freshly grated Parmesan

Soak mushrooms in warm water 20 minutes. Drain, reserving liquid. Strain liquid. Rinse mushrooms with cold water, then press to remove as much moisture as possible. Chop mushrooms coarsely, discarding any tough stems. Set mushrooms and liquid aside.

In skillet, melt butter over moderate heat. Add onion and garlic and sauté until soft. Stir in mushroom soaking liquid and bring to boil. Stir in mushrooms and season to taste with salt and pepper. Remove from heat and keep warm.

In large saucepan, cook polenta according to package directions, increasing water by about 1/2 cup (cooked polenta should be slightly runny). Season to taste with salt and pepper. Divide polenta among 4 individual serving bowls and add mascarpone to each. Stir just to swirl cheese into polenta. Top each with mushroom sauce and pass Parmesan at table.

Serves 4.

CORN & SUN-DRIED TOMATO SOUFFLÉ

2 cups corn kernels
¼ cup butter
¼ cup all-purpose flour
1¼ teaspoons coarse salt
½ teaspoon freshly ground pepper
1 cup milk
5 eggs, separated
6 to 8 oil-packed sun-dried tomatoes, chopped

Preheat oven to 350 degrees F.

Set aside 1/2 cup corn kernels. Place remaining corn in food processor or blender and process until ground. Set aside.

In saucepan, melt butter and blend in flour, salt and pepper. Stir in milk and cook, stirring frequently, until thickened.

In bowl, beat egg yolks lightly. Whisk in small amount of hot sauce, then pour eggs into pan. Cook and stir 1 minute. Remove from heat and stir in tomatoes, reserved corn kernels, and ground corn.

In bowl of mixer, beat egg whites until stiff. Fold 1/3 into corn mixture, then fold in remaining whites. Pour into 5-cup soufflé dish, place in larger pan of hot water, and bake 40 to 45 minutes. Serve immediately.

Serves 6.

GRATIN OF CORN & ZUCCHINI WITH CHIPOTLE

2 tablespoons vegetable oil
1 small onion, diced
3 cups corn kernels
2 small zucchinis, grated
2 canned chipotles, minced
1 cup shredded panela or jack cheese
2 eggs, beaten
Coarse salt and freshly ground pepper
2 stale corn tortillas, ground

Preheat oven to 400 degrees F.

In large skillet, heat oil over medium-high heat. Add onion and sauté until soft. Stir in corn, zucchini, and chipotles and cook, stirring often, 6 to 7 minutes. Remove from heat and stir in 3/4 cup cheese and eggs. Season to taste with salt and pepper.

Spread mixture in greased gratin dish or shallow casserole. Toss ground tortillas with remaining 1/4 cup cheese and sprinkle over top. Bake 20 minutes or until top is browned.

Serves 6.

CORN IN MEXICAN FOLKLORE

Since ancient times corn has been the Mexican symbol of sustenance. The Indian word maiz *means "sacred mother" or "giver of life." Among the legends surrounding the mighty plant is the belief that corn that is wasted or scattered on the ground will complain to God. Corn is afraid to be cooked, so a woman must warm it first with her breath. And cornmeal sprinkled across the doorway keeps enemies out.*

CORN TIMBALES

2 tablespoons butter
2 tablespoons all-purpose flour
3⁄4 cup condensed chicken broth
3⁄4 cup half-and-half
4 eggs, beaten
11⁄2 cups corn kernels
1⁄4 cup chopped fresh chives
1 cup shredded white cheddar or
smoked mozzarella

Preheat oven to 375 degrees F.

In skillet, melt butter over medium-high heat. Stir in flour to blend, then gradually stir in broth and half and half until smooth. Bring to boil, stirring constantly, and cook until thickened. Remove from heat and slowly stir about 1/3 mixture into eggs, then return mixture to sauce in pan and stir in corn, chives, and cheese. Cook and stir over medium heat just until cheese melts.

Spoon into 6 (6-ounce) buttered custard cups or molds. Cover with foil, set in large roasting pan, and fill with water halfway up sides of cups.

Bake 40 minutes or until knife inserted in center comes out clean. Remove cups from pan and cool on rack 10 minutes. Run sharp knife around edges to loosen and unmold onto serving plates.

Serves 6.

CREAMY CORN & FENNEL

3 tablespoons butter
1 small fennel bulb, trimmed and chopped
1 onion, diced
4 cups corn kernels
1 cup chicken broth
1/2 cup heavy cream
1/2 cup grated Parmesan
    Coarse salt and freshly ground pepper

In large skillet, melt butter over medium-high heat. Add fennel and onion and sauté 5 minutes. Add corn and broth, raise heat to high and cook, stirring, until liquid is nearly evaporated, 4 to 6 minutes. Slowly stir in cream, remove from heat, and stir in Parmesan. Season to taste with salt and pepper.

Serves 6.

CORN ON THE COB

*It is almost impossible to undercook corn on the cob.
We have even been known to nibble uncooked sweet corn
straight from the farmer's market.*

Ears of corn
Softened butter
Salt and freshly ground pepper

Bring enough water to a boil in large pot to generously
cover corn. Meanwhile remove and discard husks
and silk and rinse corn. Add cobs to water with pinch
of salt and cook 2 minutes, once water has returned to
boil. Serve immediately with pats of butter, salt, and
pepper, or cover pot and keep warm in water as long
as 20 minutes.

CORN'S TRIP AROUND THE WORLD

Though corn was introduced to Europe by Columbus in 1492, it was not immediately accepted. Europeans were dedicated wheat eaters who considered corn best left to animals. By 1525, however, Spaniards starting eating corn. Andalusia, in southern Spain, became a corn farming region. From there it traveled around the Mediterranean region and to northern Italy, where polenta became the staple food of the poor.

MEXICAN GRILLED CORN

We have developed such a passion for charred corn with chile, salt, and lime as it is eaten on the streets in Mexico that we may never boil corn cobs again. That is, until the next fourth of July.

Unhusked corn ears
Butter
Chili powder, salt, and freshly ground pepper
Lime wedges

Preheat grill and soak corn in cold water to cover, 30 minutes.

Shake off excess water and grill corn, turning frequently, until evenly charred, 20 minutes. Using a kitchen towel, pick up each ear of corn and pull back husks and silk, leaving them attached at the stem. Continue grilling, turning frequently, until evenly charred, about 7 minutes.

Meanwhile melt about 1 tablespoon butter for each ear of corn. Season butter with chile, salt, and black pepper. Generously brush all over cobs and serve each with a wedge of lime. Leave husks attached for easy handling.

CORN'S TRIP AROUND THE WORLD

The neighboring Portuguese brought it to Africa, thereby introducing a mixed blessing to that grain-poor continent. Since corn grew quickly, kept well and provided plenty of food, cornmeal became the staple, and in some cases only, food of the African poor. The ships that transported Africans to the New World carried two things—people and cornmeal to keep them alive. Corn bread and water was the steady diet of slaves in America.

CONTENTS

ENTRÉES

LOBSTER CORN SALAD

Leave it to lobster to bring simple corn and potatoes to a whole new level.

1/4 cup rice vinegar
1/4 cup olive oil
8 scallions, trimmed and thinly sliced
  Salt and freshly ground pepper
1 pound red potatoes, thinly sliced
2 cups fresh corn kernels
2 red bell peppers, roasted, peeled, seeded, and diced
1 pound cooked lobster meat, in 1/2-inch slices

Whisk together rice vinegar, oil, scallions, salt, and pepper to make dressing. Set aside.

Bring medium pot of salted water to boil. Blanch potatoes just until done, about 8 minutes. Remove with slotted spoon. Rinse with cold water, drain, and toss with half the dressing.

In the same pot of boiling water, blanch corn kernels just until water returns to boil. Strain and rinse well with cold water. Add corn and roasted red pepper to potatoes and toss well.

Divide and spoon corn mixture into 4 shallow bowls. Top each with lobster meat, drizzle with remaining dressing, and serve.

Serves 4.

"Corn is a very sacred food, because in the legends, when the corn finally comes up, the corn becomes a man. Corn comes from the earth—it's a thing that's been given to us by the Great Spirit."

—Agnes Dill of Isleta Pueblo

ROASTED CORN & TURKEY SALAD

This substantial salad blends the earthy flavors of black beans, corn chips, and smoked turkey with roasted corn.

 4 ears corn, husked and cleaned
 1 head romaine lettuce, washed and julienned
 1/2 red onion, thinly sliced
 2 plum tomatoes, in chunks
 1 (16-ounce) can black beans, washed and drained
 1/4 cup cilantro leaves
 1 pound smoked turkey breast
 1/3 cup red wine vinegar
 2/3 cup olive oil
   Salt and freshly ground black pepper
 1/2 cup crumbled feta cheese
   Fried corn tortilla chips as garnish

Grill or broil corn, turning frequently, until golden and partially charred. Set aside to cool, then scrape off kernels.

In large mixing bowl combine lettuce, onion, tomato, black beans, cilantro, and corn kernels. Toss well and refrigerate.

Trim turkey of excess fat and cut into 1/2-inch cubes. Whisk together red wine vinegar and olive oil to make vinaigrette. Season with salt and pepper.

Pour vinaigrette over salad and toss well. Sprinkle turkey and feta cheese over top and garnish with tortilla chips.

Serves 4.

THE HEALTH CONNECTION

Corn-dependent societies have traditionally suffered from pellagra, a disease caused by severe protein and mineral deficiencies. Native American Indians knew how to treat corn to improve its nutritional value by processing it with lime or ashes and planting it next to beans, which supply the very proteins lacking in corn. So smile the next time you eat tortillas and beans. You are eating some very inexpensive protein.

CHICKEN & CORN CHILI

2 tablespoons olive oil
1 pound boneless, skinless chicken breasts, diced
3 shallots, minced
3 garlic cloves, minced
1 pound tomatillos, husked and chopped
2 tomatoes, peeled and chopped
2 to 3 Anaheims, roasted, peeled, seeded, and chopped
1/2 teaspoon crumbled dried oregano
1/2 teaspoon ground coriander
1/4 teaspoon ground cumin
1 (14 1/2-ounce) can chicken broth
2 cups cooked and drained cannellini or
   white kidney beans
2 cups corn kernels
   Juice of 1 lime
   Coarse salt and freshly ground pepper
   Chopped red onion, cilantro leaves, sour cream,
   Shredded jack cheese and/or lime wedges (optional)

In large saucepan, heat olive oil over moderate heat. Add chicken and cook, stirring often, just until it begins to brown. Remove with slotted spoon and set aside.

Add shallots and garlic to pan and sauté until soft. Add tomatillos, tomatoes, chiles, oregano, coriander, and cumin and cook 5 minutes, stirring occasionally. Return chicken to pan along with broth and bring to boil. Reduce to simmer and cook about 20 minutes. Add drained beans and corn and cook just until heated through, about 5 minutes. Add lime juice and season to taste with salt and pepper. Serve with chopped red onion, cilantro, sour cream, jack cheese, and/or lime wedges to add as desired.

Serves 4.

COWBOY CASSEROLE WITH CORN DUMPLINGS

2 tablespoons vegetable oil
1 onion, diced
3 garlic cloves, minced
2 pounds lean ground beef
2 tablespoons chili powder
1 teaspoon dried oregano leaves
1/2 teaspoon ground cumin
1 (28-ounce) can chopped tomatoes
1 (7-ounce) can diced green chiles
Coarse salt and freshly ground pepper
2 cups shredded cheddar cheese
2 eggs
1/3 cup sour cream
1 (81/2-ounce) package corn muffin mix
1 cup corn kernels

Heat oil in large skillet over high heat. Add onion and garlic and sauté until translucent. Add ground beef and cook, stirring to break into chunks, until well browned. Drain any excess fat.

Sprinkle chili powder, oregano, and cumin evenly over meat mixture. Cook mixture, stirring, 30 seconds longer. Stir in tomatoes and green chiles. Season to taste with salt and pepper. Transfer mixture to 13 by 9-inch baking dish. Sprinkle with cheddar cheese.

Preheat oven to 375 degrees F. In bowl, beat eggs with sour cream just to blend. Add to muffin mix and stir just until moistened. Fold in corn. Drop by rounded spoonfuls over casserole, spacing evenly. Bake 30 to 35 minutes, or until dumplings begin to brown and sauce is bubbling. Remove from oven and let stand about 10 minutes before serving.

Serves 8.

WHITE CORN ENCHILADAS VERDES

2 (18-ounce) cans tomatillos, drained
1 (7-ounce) can diced green chiles
1 onion, chopped
2 garlic cloves, chopped
1/2 cup cilantro leaves
1 (14 1/2-ounce) can chicken broth
Oil
Coarse salt
3 cups white corn kernels
1 cup crumbled cotija or feta cheese
12 corn tortillas
1 1/2 cups shredded jack cheese

In food processor, purée tomatillos, chiles, onion, garlic, cilantro, and 3⁄4 cup chicken broth.

In large skillet, heat 2 tablespoons oil over medium-high heat. Add purée and cook 5 minutes, stirring frequently. Slowly stir in remaining broth and cook 10 minutes longer, or until thickened. Season to taste with salt.

In bowl, combine corn and cotija. Add 1 cup tomatillo sauce and stir to combine. Set aside.

Preheat oven to 350 degrees F. In another skillet, heat 1⁄4 inch oil over medium-high heat to 400 degrees F. Fry tortillas, one at a time, just until soft. With tongs, transfer each to sauce, turning to coat both sides, and place on plate. Spoon corn filling down center of each and roll to enclose. Arrange in 13 by 9-inch baking dish, repeating until all tortillas are filled. Spoon remaining sauce over all. Sprinkle with jack cheese and bake 25 minutes.

Serves 4 to 6.

POZOLE

This is a spicy, red-chile version of pozole, the traditional Mexican stew of pork and hominy. Serve with plenty of warm tortillas and cold beer.

1 ancho chile, wiped clean
1/4 cup vegetable oil
2 pounds boneless pork loin, in 1-inch cubes
    Salt and freshly ground black pepper
1 onion, diced
4 garlic cloves, minced
2 quarts chicken stock
1 tablespoon dried oregano
2 teaspoons cracked black peppercorns
2 (15-ounce) cans white hominy, drained and rinsed
1/2 head cabbage, thickly shredded
    Lime wedges for garnish

Briefly roast ancho chile over gas flame until soft and fragrant. Place in bowl with boiling water to cover and let soak 20 minutes. Remove seeds and purée with about 1/2 cup soaking liquid. Set aside.

Heat oil in large heavy pot over medium heat. Season pork all over with salt and pepper and then brown in oil. Remove with slotted spoon. Sauté onion, garlic, and ancho chile purée 5 minutes and return pork to pot. Pour in stock, oregano, pepper, and salt, as desired. Bring to boil, reduce to simmer, and cook until meat is tender, about 2 hours.

Stir in hominy and cabbage. Simmer 10 minutes longer and serve hot in soup bowls with lime wedges as garnish.

Serves 6 to 8.

FISH & CORN CALDO

Caldos are the big, rich, soupy stews of Mexico. This one makes a heart-warming dinner with a loaf of French bread.

3 tablespoons olive oil
1 onion, chopped
4 garlic cloves, minced
2 tomatoes, seeded and diced
4 cups fish stock or clam juice
2 small boiling potatoes, unpeeled, cut in chunks
2 ears corn, cleaned and cut into 1/2-inch slices
1 teaspoon dried oregano
2 pounds white fish fillets, such as flounder,
    sea bass, or red snapper, cut into 2-inch chunks
    Salt and freshly ground pepper
    Juice of 1 lime
1 to 2 jalapeños, seeded and minced
1/2 cup fresh cilantro leaves
    Lime wedges for garnish

Heat oil over medium-high heat in non-aluminum stockpot. Sauté onion and garlic until golden. Add tomato and continue cooking, stirring frequently, 5 minutes longer.

Pour in fish stock, along with potatoes, corn, and oregano. Bring to boil, reduce to simmer, and cook 20 minutes.

Add fish chunks and bring back to boil. Reduce to simmer and cook, covered, until fish is opaque, about 10 minutes. Season with salt and pepper to taste. Add remaining ingredients and serve in soup bowls with additional lime wedges to be used at table.

Serves 4.

"There are hundreds of accounts of American farmers who say they have heard their corn growing. On a warm windless evening during the peak growing time, you can sit in a cornfield and hear the earth and the vegetable kingdom at work: a gentle stroke and rasp of leaves unfurling . . .

—Margaret Visser

SHRIMP WITH CORN & PEPPERS

1 tablespoon butter
1 each green, red, and yellow bell pepper, stemmed, seeded, and sliced
1 onion, thinly sliced
1 pound large shrimp, peeled and deveined
1 1/2 cups corn kernels
1 (14-ounce) can chopped tomatoes
2 teaspoons mixed dried Italian herbs, such as oregano, basil, and rosemary
1/2 cup heavy cream
Coarse salt and freshly ground pepper

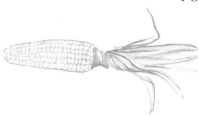

In large skillet, melt butter over medium heat. Add peppers and onion and cook 2 minutes. Add shrimp, corn, tomatoes, and Italian herbs and bring to boil. Reduce heat and simmer 3 minutes. Stir in cream and heat through. Serve over pasta or rice.

Serves 4 to 6.

CORN FOR THE KETTLE

The American standard for boiling corn is corn whose husks are green and whose kernels exude milk when pressed with a thumbnail. Fresh sweet corn is also known as "green corn" and it was the Europeans who taught the Indians to boil rather than roast it. The ideal scenario relies on rushing fresh-picked ears to a kettle of boiling water, preferably set up in the cornfield, for maximum sweetness.

For those of us who must rely on the supermarket or farmer's market for our green corn, look for ears with husks attached. Store it in the vegetable bin of the refrigerator until cooking time. To check for worms without removing husks, squeeze ears firmly in the palm of your hand and feel for hollow spots, where kernels may be eaten away.

FRESH CORN SCRAMBLE

Though corn grows in a wide variety of colors, to the modern American palate, sweet, young yellow or white kernels taste best. Yellow dent has replaced most of the Indian varieties except blue corn of the Southwest.

2 tablespoons olive oil
1/2 cup diced onion
2 garlic cloves, minced
1/2 cup diced ham
2 cups corn kernels
2 cups chopped spinach leaves
8 eggs
1/4 cup grated Parmesan
Dried red pepper flakes, coarse salt, and freshly ground pepper

Heat oil in medium skillet over medium-high heat. Add onion and cook, stirring often, until translucent. Stir in garlic and ham and cook 1 minute longer. Add corn and cook 3 minutes longer, stirring once or twice. Stir in spinach and cook just until wilted.

Beat eggs with Parmesan and add to pan. When beginning to set, stir gently then continue to cook, stirring occasionally until set. Season to taste with red pepper flakes, salt, and pepper.

Serves 6 to 8.

The color of the husks and silk indicates corn's age. Pale golden silks and green husks mean immature, sweet corn for boiling; a shade darker means corn for roasting; and even darker indicates dryer corn for grinding. Blackened husks means hard feed for animals. Corn is useful as food at each stage of its life.

STUFFED RED PEPPERS

4 red bell peppers, halved
  lengthwise and seeded
2 tablespoons olive oil
1 small onion, diced
4 garlic cloves, minced
1 large tomato, chopped
2 cups corn kernels
1/4 cup chopped black olives
2 tablespoons chopped fresh basil
1 cup ricotta cheese
  Coarse salt and freshly
  ground pepper
1/2 cup shredded mozzarella
4 large basil leaves

Preheat oven to 350 degrees F.

Drop pepper halves into boiling salted water and cook 5 minutes. Drain and set aside.

In large skillet, heat oil over medium-high heat. Add onion and cook until soft. Add garlic and cook 30 seconds longer. Stir in tomato, corn, olives, and basil. Cook 5 minutes, stirring once or twice. Remove from heat and stir in ricotta cheese. Season to taste with salt and pepper.

Stuff mixture into prepared pepper halves and arrange in greased 13 by 9-inch baking pan. Cover with foil and bake 15 minutes. Remove cover, sprinkle with mozzarella and bake 5 minutes longer. Garnish each with a basil leaf.

Serves 4.

STIR-FRIED BEEF WITH BABY CORN & TOMATOES

    1 tablespoon cornstarch
    1 tablespoon sugar
    ¼ cup beef broth
    2 tablespoons sherry
    2 tablespoons soy sauce
    ¼ teaspoon black pepper
    2 tablespoons oil
    ¾ pound flank steak, thinly sliced
    1 medium onion, cut in narrow wedges
    3 garlic cloves, minced
    1 jalapeño, stemmed and thinly sliced
    1 (15-ounce) can baby corn on cob, drained
       and cut into 1-inch lengths
    2 medium tomatoes, cut in 8 wedges each
       Hot cooked rice

In small bowl, combine cornstarch and sugar. Stir in broth, sherry, soy sauce, and pepper. Set aside.

In wok or large skillet, heat oil over high heat. Stir-fry steak until browned. Transfer to platter with slotted spoon. Add onion and stir-fry until beginning to brown. Stir in garlic and jalapeño and cook 1 minute longer. Add corn and cooked meat.

Swirl prepared broth mixture, pour into wok, and stir to coat ingredients. Stir in tomatoes. Cook, stirring often, until sauce is thickened, about 1 minute. Serve over rice.

Serves 4.

BOTANICALLY SPEAKING

Zea mais, the world's most efficient industrial crop, is categorized as a giant grass. Each kernel is a seed but, unlike other grasses, a seed that needs man to help it grow. Left to its own devices, corn will not reproduce.

SALMON ON A BED OF HERBED CORN

This dish fulfills all of our requirements for dinner party food. It's light, elegant, delicious, and takes no time to prepare.

3 tablespoons butter
2 ears corn kernels
   Salt and pepper
2 tablespoons chopped fresh tarragon,
   thyme, or parsley
2 tablespoons lemon juice
2 tomatoes, chopped
1 garlic clove, minced
1 tablespoon chopped fresh basil
2 tablespoons olive oil
4 (6-ounce) salmon fillets

Melt butter in small pan over medium heat. Cook corn with salt and pepper, stirring frequently, about 4 minutes. Stir in herbs and lemon juice, cook 2 minutes longer, and remove from heat.

In small bowl, combine tomatoes, garlic, basil, salt, and pepper. Set aside.

Heat oil in large skillet over high heat. Season fish all over with salt and pepper and sauté about 2 minutes per side, until done to taste. Divide corn mixture and arrange in center of each plate. Top each with salmon fillet and spoon on fresh tomato mixture. Serve hot.

Serves 4.

CORN'S LONGEVITY

Corn, preserved by drying or pickling, has an incredibly long shelf life. Archaeologists have been able to pop 1,000-year-old popcorn.

CONTENTS

GLORIOUS
CORN BREADS

BIG BUTTERMILK CORN MUFFINS

1 egg
1 cup buttermilk
2 tablespoons melted butter
3/4 cup all-purpose flour
3/4 cup yellow cornmeal
2 teaspoons baking soda
1 teaspoon baking powder
1/2 teaspoon salt

Preheat oven to 425 degrees F.

In bowl, beat egg with buttermilk and butter to blend. In separate bowl, combine flour, cornmeal, baking soda, baking powder, and salt. Stir in liquid mixture until just blended.

Spoon batter into 4 greased extra-large muffin cups. Bake 20 minutes or until cake tester inserted in center comes out clean.

Makes 4.

"People have tried and they have tried but sex is not better than sweet corn."

—Garrison Keillor

WHITE SKILLET CORN BREAD

1½ cups white cornmeal
¾ cup all-purpose flour
1 tablespoon baking powder
1 tablespoon sugar
½ teaspoon salt
2 eggs
¼ cup melted butter
1 cup beer
1 cup white corn kernels

Place 10-inch cast-iron skillet in oven. Preheat oven to 425 degrees F.

In large bowl, combine cornmeal, flour, baking powder, sugar, and salt.

In separate bowl, beat eggs with 3 tablespoons butter and beer to blend. Add to dry ingredients along with corn and stir just until dry ingredients are moistened.

Remove skillet from oven and add remaining butter, swirling to coat bottom of pan. Pour batter in hot pan and bake 20 to 25 minutes. To serve, cut into wedges.

Serves 8.

STAFF OF LIFE

Until the middle of the nineteenth century, corn bread was the standard American bread. It took the form of johnnycakes in New England, pone and dodger in the Midwest, and pone, cracklin' corn breads, muffins, and sticks in the South. In addition to their golden color, grainy texture, and corn flavor, all corn breads are relatively flat since cornmeal does not contain gluten, the protein that causes bread to rise.

HERB CORN BREAD

*This easy, hand-mixed corn bread with herbs
and a touch of cheddar cheese is excellent spread
with honey.*

 1 cup yellow cornmeal
 1 cup all-purpose flour
 1 teaspoon baking powder
1½ teaspoons salt
 ½ stick butter, melted
 2 eggs
 1 cup milk
 ½ cup grated cheddar cheese
 2 tablespoons chopped fresh herbs, such as
    tarragon, parsley, thyme, basil, oregano
    Fresh kernels from 1 cob, about ¾ cup

Preheat oven to 425 degrees F. Coat an 8-inch square or 9-inch round baking pan with butter.

Combine cornmeal, flour, baking powder, and salt in large bowl. Mix with fork.

In another bowl, whisk together melted butter, eggs, and milk. Pour into dry ingredients and mix with wooden spoon. Stir in herbs, cheese, and corn just to combine. Spoon and smooth into pan. Bake 25 minutes, until pick inserted in center comes out clean. Set aside 10 minutes to cool. Serve from pan.

Makes 1 loaf, or 8 servings.

CORN GRIDDLE CAKES

1 cup yellow cornmeal
1/4 cup all-purpose flour
1/2 teaspoon baking soda
1/2 teaspoon salt
1 egg, beaten
3/4 cup milk
1/2 cup sour cream
1 1/2 cups corn kernels
   Butter, syrup, and/or jam

In large bowl, combine cornmeal, flour, soda, and salt.

In separate bowl, combine egg, milk, and sour cream. Pour over dry ingredients and mix just until moistened. Fold in corn.

Heat griddle or large skillet over medium-high heat. Grease lightly. Ladle batter onto pan to make 4-inch cakes. Cook until brown on both sides. Serve immediately with butter, syrup, and/or jam.

Makes about 12 (4-inch) cakes, or 4 servings.

CORNMEAL WAFFLES

1 cup yellow cornmeal
1 cup all-purpose flour
2 tablespoons sugar
4 teaspoons baking powder
1/2 teaspoon salt
2 eggs, lightly beaten
13/4 cups milk
1/3 cup melted butter
Butter and berry-flavored syrup or jam

In large bowl, combine cornmeal, flour, sugar, baking powder, and salt.

In separate bowl, beat eggs with milk and butter. Add to dry ingredients and mix to blend. Pour onto hot, greased waffle iron and bake until browned and crisp. Serve with butter and syrup or jam.

Serves 6.

FRESH CORN FRITTERS

2 cups corn kernels
2 tablespoons sugar
1 teaspoon salt
3 eggs, separated
1/4 cup all-purpose flour
1/2 teaspoon baking powder
   Oil for deep frying
   Additional sugar

In food processor, combine corn, sugar, and salt. Pulse just until mixed and corn is crushed. Add egg yolks, flour, and baking powder and process just to blend. Transfer to bowl.

In mixer bowl, beat egg whites until stiff. Fold 1/3 whites into corn mixture, then fold in remaining whites.

In deep skillet or fryer, heat oil to 375 degrees F. Drop batter by tablespoons and fry, turning once, until golden. Drain on paper towels. Sprinkle with sugar and serve immediately.

Serves 6.

CORN TORTILLAS

1 cup masa harina or corn flour for tortillas
1/2 cup warm water

Place dry cast iron skillet or griddle over high heat
for 15 minutes.

Meanwhile stir together masa harina and water
in bowl with a spoon. Press together to form a moist,
smooth ball. Divide into 8 pieces and roll each between
palms to form balls.

When skillet is hot, start pressing out balls on a
tortilla press lined with plastic wrap. Cook each about
30 seconds per side, pressing with spatula to make
dough puff before turning. Stack finished tortillas
on kitchen towel and wrap to keep warm. Wrap in
aluminum foil to store in refrigerator or freezer.

Makes 8 (4-inch) tortillas.

CORN BREAD SAUSAGE STUFFING

Thanksgiving just wouldn't be the same without the best stuffing of them all—corn bread.

- 2 tablespoons olive oil
- 1 onion, chopped
- 2 celery ribs, chopped
- 4 ounces domestic mushrooms, roughly chopped
- 4 garlic cloves, minced
- 1/2 pound pork or turkey sausage, removed from casings
- 3 cups cubed corn bread
- 1/2 cup roughly chopped pecans
- 3 tablespoons chopped fresh sage
- 1/4 cup chopped fresh Italian parsley
- 1 egg, beaten
- 1 cup chicken stock
  Salt and freshly ground pepper

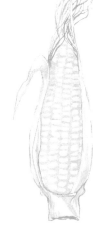

Heat oil in medium skillet over medium heat. Sauté onion, celery, and garlic until soft, about 8 minutes. Add mushrooms and cook, stirring frequently, until wilted. Crumble in sausage meat and cook, breaking up lumps with wooden spoon, until just done. Season generously with salt and pepper, drain any excess fat, and transfer to mixing bowl.

Add remaining ingredients to sausage mixture and mix well. Spoon into turkey or small ovenproof casserole and cover with foil. Bake 30 minutes at 425 degrees F., if baking alone.

Makes enough for one 12-pound turkey, or 6 servings.

"Grits is grits. There's not a whole lot of range to them."

—Roy Blount, Jr.

CONTENTS

CANDIED CORN & OTHER GROWN-UP SWEETS

CANDIED CORN KERNELS

    2 cups corn kernels
1½ cups sugar
    1 cup water

In large skillet, combine corn, 1 cup sugar, and water.
Cook over medium heat, stirring occasionally until
corn is deep golden, 45 to 60 minutes. Drain, then roll
in remaining sugar. Spread in single layer on baking
sheet and cool. Store in tightly sealed plastic bag or
container. Use as a topping for ice cream, in puddings,
custards, or fillings or as a substitute for nuts in
baked desserts.

Makes 2 cups.

CANDIED CORN TOFFEE

    3/4 cup margarine
    1/4 cup butter
     3 tablespoons water
     2 cups sugar
    1/2 teaspoon salt
    1/2 teaspoon vanilla
     1 (12-ounce) package semi-sweet chocolate morsels
     1 cup Candied Corn Kernels (see opposite page)

In large skillet combine margarine, butter, water,
sugar, salt, and vanilla. Cook and stir over medium-
high heat until mixture turns light tan. Pour mixture
into 15 by 10-inch baking pan. Immediately sprinkle
with chocolate morsels. When chocolate turns glossy,
spread evenly over toffee and sprinkle with Candied
Corn, pressing lightly into chocolate with palms.
Cool overnight, then break into pieces.

Makes about 3 pounds.

CANDIED CORN
CRÈME BRÛLÉE

8 egg yolks
3/4 cup granulated sugar
4 cups half and half
1 teaspoon vanilla
1 cup Candied Corn Kernels (see p. 86)
1/2 cup packed light brown sugar

Preheat oven to 300 degrees F.

In bowl, beat yolks with granulated sugar.

In saucepan, heat half and half to scalding. Whisk into yolk mixture. Stir in vanilla and corn. Pour mixture into 8 (6-ounce) ramekins or custard cups. Place in roasting pan and pour hot water in pan, halfway up sides of ramekins. Loosely cover with foil and bake 1 hour or until custards are set. Remove dishes from pan and cool on rack. Cover and chill.

Preheat broiler. Place ramekins on baking sheet and sprinkle each evenly with brown sugar. Cook under broiler until sugar melts, about 30 seconds, watching carefully to prevent burning. Serve immediately.

Serves 8.

CORN CRÊPES WITH BERRY COULIS

3 eggs, beaten
1 teaspoon salt
1/2 cup sugar
1 cup all-purpose flour
1 1/2 cups milk
1/4 cup melted butter
Additional butter for pan
1 1/2 cups boysenberries or raspberries
1 1/2 cups Candied Corn Kernels (see p. 86)

In bowl, beat eggs with salt and 1 tablespoon sugar. Whisk in flour, milk, and melted butter. Allow to stand at least 1 hour or refrigerate overnight.

Brush crêpe or small sauté pan lightly with butter and heat over medium-high heat. Spoon scant ¼ cup batter in pan and tip to evenly coat. Cook 1 minute, jerk pan to loosen crêpe, and turn and cook other side 20 to 30 seconds. Repeat, brushing pan lightly with butter as needed, and stacking crêpes with waxed paper between each.

In small saucepan, combine berries and remaining sugar. Bring to boil, then remove from heat and cool slightly. If desired, mixture can be puréed and strained.

To serve, briefly reheat crêpes in pan. Place on plate and sprinkle evenly with Candied Corn Kernels. Fold in quarters or roll up. Place 2 crêpes on each plate and spoon berry coulis over top.

Serves 6 to 8.

CORN MADELEINES

1 cup all-purpose flour
1 cup yellow cornmeal
1/4 cup sugar
1 tablespoon baking powder
1/2 teaspoon salt
1 egg
1 cup milk
1/4 cup melted butter
Additional butter and cornmeal

Preheat oven to 375 degrees F.

In bowl, combine flour, cornmeal, sugar, baking powder, and salt.

In separate bowl, beat egg with milk and butter. Stir milk mixture into dry ingredients just until moistened.

Butter madeleine pans generously and sprinkle lightly with cornmeal. Spoon butter into pans, filling each mold to the rim.

Bake 10 to 15 minutes or until madeleines spring back when pressed with finger. Cool in pans 5 minutes, then invert pans and release, using sharp knife to loosen, if necessary. Serve warm or at room temperature.

Makes about 2 dozen.

corny **1**. *of or abounding in corn.* **2**. *old-fashioned; lacking in subtlety and full of clichés* **3**. *mawkishly sentimental*

CRISPY CORNMEAL WAFERS

These are perfect with tea or a glass of lemonade.

    ¾ cup confectioners' sugar
    1 stick butter, softened
      Grated zest of 1 lemon
    ¾ cup flour
    ¾ cup yellow cornmeal
    ¼ teaspoon salt

Preheat oven to 350 degrees F. Cream together sugar, butter, and lemon zest until light and fluffy.

In another bowl, mix together cornmeal, flour, and salt with a fork. Add dry ingredients to creamed mixture and beat well to combine. Press dough together to form a ball.

On lightly floured surface with floured rolling pin, roll out dough to ¼-inch thickness. Cut out cookies with cookie cutter or small juice glass dipped in flour. Place about 1 inch apart on uncoated cookie sheets. Bake 18 to 20 minutes, until golden brown along edges. Carefully transfer to racks to cool. Gather up excess dough, roll again, cut out, and bake until all dough is used.

Makes about 18 cookies.

CARAMEL POPCORN

2½ quarts popped corn
1 cup mixed nuts
¼ cup butter
1 cup light brown sugar
½ cup light corn syrup
⅔ cup sweetened condensed milk
1 teaspoon vanilla

In large metal bowl, combine popped corn and nuts. Set aside.

In saucepan, combine butter, sugar, and corn syrup. Bring to boil over medium heat. Stir in condensed milk, reduce heat, and simmer, stirring consistently, until mixture registers 245 degrees F. on candy thermometer or when drop forms firm but pliable ball in cold water. Remove from heat and stir in vanilla. Immediately pour caramel mixture over popcorn mixture in bowl and toss to coat. Butter hands lightly and press into 1-inch pieces. Set aside to cool.

Makes about 3 quarts.

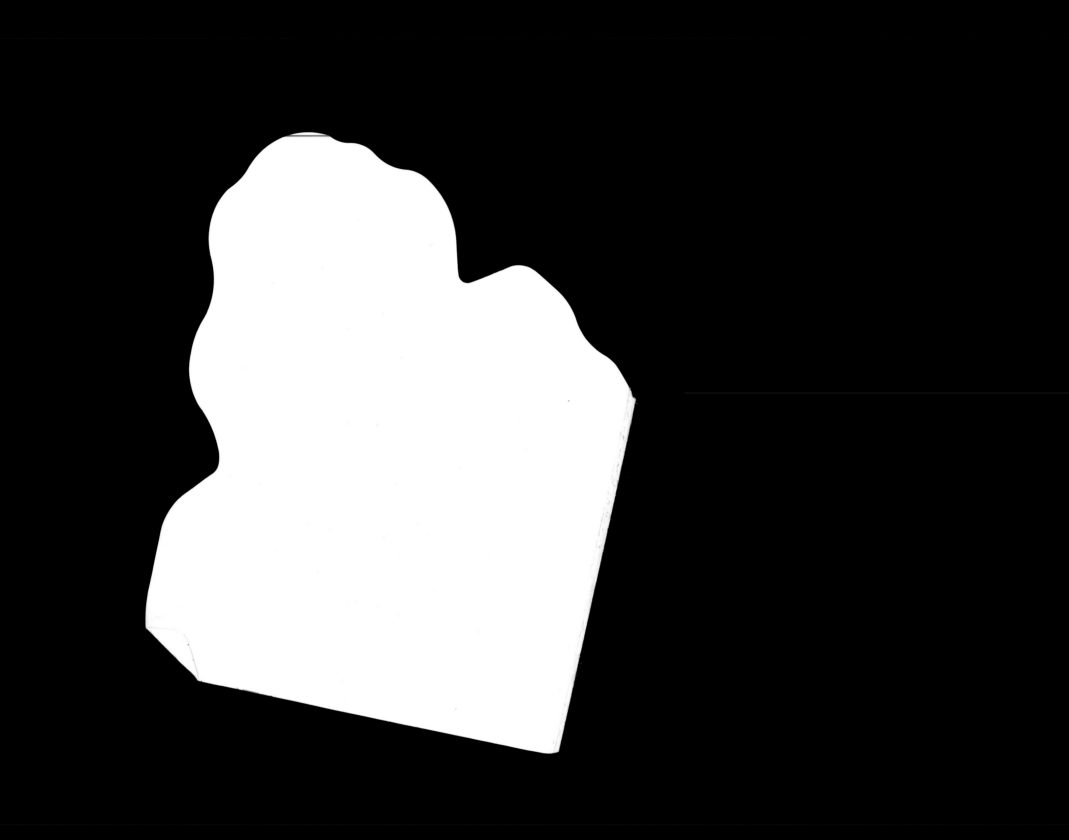